Gloria!

Letters From Hymnwriters

Ruth M. Buenting

CSS Publishing Company, Inc., Lima, Ohio

GLORIA!

Copyright © 1999 by
CSS Publishing Company, Inc.
Lima, Ohio

The original purchaser may photocopy material in this publication for use as it was intended (i.e. worship material for worship use; educational material for classroom use; dramatic material for staging or production). No additional permission is required from the publisher for such copying by the original purchaser only. Inquiries should be addressed to: Permissions, CSS Publishing Company, Inc. P.O. Box 4503, Lima, Ohio 45802-4503.

Library of Congress Cataloging-in-Publication Data

Buenting, Ruth M., 1944-
   Gloria: letters from the hymn writers/Ruth M. Buenting.
     p.   cm.
   ISBN 0-7880-1526-5 (pbk. : alk. paper)
   1. Hymn writers Biography. 2. Imaginary letters.   I. Title.
BV325.B84   1999
264'.23'0922—dc21   99-37621
                                                                              CIP

ISBN 0-7880-1526-5   PRINTED IN U.S.A.

*With many thanks to my husband, James,
for his encouragement and patience*

and to

*J. Robert Jacobson
First Bishop of Alberta and the Territories,
Evangelical Lutheran Church in Canada
for his suggestions and assistance*

In memory of my parents

*Anna-Mae Miller Wellman
and
Arthur Thomas Wellman*

My mother, who with Frances Havergal said, "We love,"

and

My dad, who with Samuel Medley said, "He lives."

Preface

As I began to research the stories of the hymnwriters, it was their faith which *amazed* me the most. How could they keep praising God when many times their circumstances were other than pleasant?

By God's abundant grace, people like Martin Rinckart wrote NOW THANK WE ALL OUR GOD when most of us would have been writing a hymn with quite a different text. But that was Pastor Martin's prayer!

Or read the "letter" from Horatio Spafford. How could he ever write a hymn of peace, WHEN PEACE LIKE A RIVER, during such a tragedy? Spafford was obviously leaving the "why" to God himself.

Or reflect on Nikolai Grundtvig's message found in BUILT ON A ROCK. The Spirit of God was with him as he confronted the "age of reason" with faith in Jesus Christ.

The hymnwriters have left to us more than hymns. They have left us a legacy of faith and prayers bound up in their hymns. These hymns point the way to Christ. The stories are theirs.

After decades and hundreds of years, their songs of praise continue to reecho in our era. For we too can *identify* in our darkness as well as in our joy with these people of prayer ... the hymnwriters.

> *All praise and thanks to God*
> *The Father now be given,*
> *The Son, and him who reigns*
> *With them in highest heaven,*
> *The one eternal God,*
> *Whom earth and heav'n adore;*
> *For thus it was, is now,*
> *And shall be evermore.*
> — Martin Rinckart

Ruth Buenting
March 1999

Foreword

There are times like our own when the musical life of the Church expands so remarkably that it fairly explodes! There are many new expressions alongside a rich heritage of Christian song glorifying God through centuries.

In order that nothing may be lost, Ruth M. Buenting has provided an accessible and devotional resource chiefly on hymns of European origin. A hymn by a different writer has been selected for each Sunday of the Church Year as well as major festivals. In order to share insight regarding the faith and life of the writer as well as the inspiration for the hymn's text we receive a "letter" from the writer. Some writers also "comment" on how their original work has been used, translated, or modified over time. The faithful witness to Christ of poets and musicians and the enduring quality of many of their texts is evident in these tributes. Whether a specific hymn or its writer is better or lesser known, each makes a contribution to the worship life of the universal church out of their own background and tradition.

We are reminded of Jesus' words about the kingdom of God being like a householder who brings out treasures which are new and old (Matthew 13:52). May the worship of Christ's Church reflect this wisdom as the reign of God comes nearer.

The Reverend Richard Stetson
Assistant to the Bishop (Worship)
Evangelical Lutheran Church in Canada
Second Sunday in Lent, 1999

Table Of Contents

Advent 1 — Philipp Nicolai	13
Advent 2 — Johannes Olearius	14
Advent 3 — Paul Gerhardt	15
Advent 4 — Phillip Doddridge	17
Christmas Eve — Joseph Mohr	18
Christmas Day — Isaac Watts	19
Christmas 1 — James Montgomery	20
The Name of Jesus — John Newton	22
Epiphany Day — William Chatterton Dix	23
Epiphany 1 — Christopher Wordsworth	24
Epiphany 2 — Frank Mason North	25
Epiphany 3 — Elisabeth Cruciger	26
Epiphany 4 — William Arthur Dunkerley	27
Epiphany 5 — Mary Ann Thomson	28
Epiphany 6 — Johann Heermann	29
Transfiguration Sunday — Joseph Robinson	30
Ash Wednesday — Nikolaus Decius	31

Lent 1 — Martin Luther	33
Lent 2 — Thomas Kingo	34
Lent 3 — Nicolaus Ludwig von Zinzendorf	35
Lent 4 — Elizabeth Cecelia Clephane	36
Lent 5 — Erdmann Neumeister	37
Palm Sunday — Henry Milman	39
Maundy Thursday — Johann Rist	40
Good Friday — Cecil Frances Humphreys Alexander	41
Easter Sunday — Christian Fuerchtegott Gellert	42
Easter 2 — Samuel Medley	44
Easter 3 — Birgitte Katerine Boye	45
Easter 4 — Henry W. Baker	47
Easter 5 — John Macleod Campbell Crum	49
Easter 6 — Ulrik Vilhelm Koren	50
Ascension Day — Thomas Kelly	52
Easter 7 — Frances Ridley Havergal	53
Pentecost — Timothy Rees	55
Trinity Sunday — Reginald Heber	56
Pentecost 2 — Henry Lyte	58

Pentecost 3 — Julie von Hausmann	60
Pentecost 4 — Maltbie Davenport Babcock	61
Pentecost 5 — Charles Wesley	63
Pentecost 6 — Joachim Neander	64
Pentecost 7 — Horatius Bonar	66
Pentecost 8 — Johann Franck	67
Pentecost 9 — Carl Gustaf Boberg	69
Pentecost 10 — John Ernest Bode	70
Pentecost 11 — Georg Neumark	71
Pentecost 12 — Bates Burt	72
Pentecost 13 — Karolina Wilhelmina Berg	74
Pentecost 14 — Horatio G. Spafford	75
Pentecost 15 — John Douglas Sutherland Campbell	76
Pentecost 16 — Benjamin Schmolck	77
Pentecost 17 — William Williams	78
Pentecost 18 — George Croly	79
Pentecost 19 — William Walsham How	80
Pentecost 20 — Martin Rinckart	81
Pentecost 21 — Matthias Claudius	82

Reformation Sunday — Nikolai Grundtvig   83
    (Pentecost 22)

All Saints' Sunday — John Athelstan Laurie Riley   84
    (Pentecost 23)

Pentecost 24 — Johann Michael Altenberg   85

Pentecost 25 — Johann Burkhard Freystein   87

Christ The King Sunday — Edward Perronet   88

Advent 1   **Philipp Nicolai**

Dear People of Christ,

Have you ever thought of *joy* in the middle of a chaotic situation? I must tell you that if it had not been for thoughts of joy, I would have never survived during the time I was pastor in Unna, Westphalia, Germany.

I only lived there for a short period. However, when I lived there, a vicious plague tore through the city, leaving 1300 people dead in just seven months!

It was under such conditions in 1598 that I was writing *Mirror of Joy*. This was a series of meditations on eternal life. Because I kept my mind and spirit focused on the life of the world to come, I found peace and joy in the worst of circumstances.

Nevertheless, I had my share of heartaches during this time. For my beloved pupil, Wilhelm Ernst, died at the age of fifteen. The youth's death affected me greatly. As a result, I wrote two hymns with accompanying melodies, dedicating them to him. It was only with God's help that I survived this great loss.

The verses of these hymns begin with initials of his name or with his full titled name of nobility. In WAKE, AWAKE, FOR NIGHT IS FLYING, I have used just his simple name, reversing the initials which begin the three stanzas.

In the end, I survived the plague. *Mirror of Joy* was published and appended with these two hymns. Eventually, WAKE, AWAKE, FOR NIGHT IS FLYING became known as the "King of Chorales" or the "King of Hymns" in Germany. It still is known as that today.

However, most people do not know it was written under less than joyful circumstances. What's the secret of surviving the troubled times in our lives?

Inner joy, found only in God's Spirit.

                                                        Philipp Nicolai
                                                          (1556-1608)

Advent 2 — Johannes Olearius

Dear People in Christ,

What a comfort are our hymns of faith. Our family has found both contentment and consolation in them in the good times and in bad times. We have sung them and etched them in our hearts.

While on my earthly journey, my large hymnal was published in Leipzig, Germany. It contained over 1200 hymns. One of the largest collections of German hymns of that century, nearly 300 found in this song book are mine.

However, I am not the only hymnwriter in our family. My father also wrote hymns. One of my best-known hymns is another Advent hymn, COMFORT, COMFORT NOW MY PEOPLE.

And what a comfort it is to know that Christ will return someday, and that we will dwell with Him in His Courts. There can be no greater comfort than to dwell with Christ, the Lamb of God.

Have you ever given any thought to the word *comfort*? That we should comfort one another is to do the will of our Lord. People still are in need of much comfort today, as people through the centuries have always been in need of it. You might say it is *holy medicine*.

I believe you could call this word *comfort* also by another name, *empathy*. This is something that cannot be learned in a structured course. You cannot buy it either. Comfort can only come from God's Holy Spirit dwelling within you. For He will give you the right words to say at the right time.

As you get older, the Bible verses and hymn stanzas that you learned in your youth will *comfort* you when no one is around. Perhaps you are not old, but lonely. In these verses and stanzas you can still find comfort in today's often hectic world. These can never be taken away from you. For they are yours forever.

What a *comforting* thought.

Johannes Olearius
(1611-1684)

Advent 3   **Paul Gerhardt**

Dear People in Christ, our loving Savior,

    As a young man, I went to Wittenberg to study theology, wanting very much to become a Lutheran pastor. I remained there for fourteen long years.

    You see, my studies were constantly interrupted because of the Thirty Years' War. After I had completed my education, it was difficult to secure a parish. There were times when I thought I would stay in Wittenberg forever.

    By 1657, I was appointed as a pastor of St. Nicholas' Church in Berlin. I was there for ten years. However, the intolerant Reformed Grand Duke eventually issued a statement. All Lutheran pastors were required to sign this document saying that they would not preach against doctrinal differences.

    More trouble. As I would not sign the document, my position was cancelled. Two years passed. I was assigned to a church in Lueben, a very difficult parish.

    During this time, I encountered personal difficulties as well. I lost nearly my whole family. All our children died except for one. And only a year after I had been dismissed from St. Nicholas' Church, my precious wife, Anna Maria, died. We were married for only thirteen years. I was left to raise our one son alone.

    But whatever the conditions, I found peace in writing approximately 130 hymns. Through the years, people have said that they stand out from any others that were ever written in Germany. They say that these hymns shine with linguistic beauty and sheer simplicity.

    But for me, my hymns mirror my deep trust in God and the hope of salvation through Christ Jesus. The composers, Johann Crüger and Johann Ebeling, adorned this religious poetry with exquisite melodies.

    Perhaps you have heard of my Advent hymn, O LORD, HOW SHALL I MEET YOU. In any and all circumstances, the Lord was always there for me. All I had to do was to meet Him in worship and in prayer.

Is that where you meet Him, too?

> *O Lord, how shall I meet you,*
> *How welcome you aright?*
> *Your people long to greet you,*
> *My hope, my heart's delight!*
> *O kindle, Lord most holy,*
> *Your lamp within my breast*
> *To do in spirit lowly*
> *All that may please you best.*

Paul Gerhardt
(1607-1676)

Advent 4   **Philip Doddridge**

Dear People of Christ,

    I am delighted that my hymn HARK THE GLAD SOUND! is still being sung. I had no idea that the hymns I wrote to illustrate my sermons would ever be published.

    During my lifetime, I copied them out for members of my congregation as well as friends. I gave them out freely. However, these hymns were published four years after I entered the realm of the heavenly kingdom. Approximately 400 flowed from my pen.

    I was the last of twenty children. In your mind, you probably envision a large active household. But this was not the case. I had only one sibling. The other eighteen did not live beyond infancy. As the last child, my parents were older and left me orphaned at an early age.

    The Duchess of Bedford offered to educate me at Cambridge in order that I could be a clergyman in the Church of England. However, I chose Jenning's Dissenting Academy in Kibworth instead. These institutions were an alternative to universities at the time for nonconformist students.

    Completing my schooling, I ministered in Kibworth for six years. Then I moved on to the congregation at Castle Hill Meeting in Northampton. Here I remained until my death.

    On the advice of Isaac Watts, I founded a dissenting academy in 1729 at Market Harborough. In addition to my pastoral duties, I also taught at this new academy. I had classes in Hebrew, Greek, algebra, and trigonometry, as well as many other subjects.

    HARK THE GLAD SOUND! was also used to illustrate one of my Christmas sermons. However, I understand it is now used in the Season of Advent. *Advent* is the beginning of the church year.

    I have thought much about my beginning. Years ago, I realized I owed a debt of gratitude to God for letting me live. I listened to *the sound* of His voice. In listening to God's voice, I knew I was here for a purpose.

    And so are you.

                                                         Philip Doddridge
                                                              (1702-1751)

Christmas Eve   **Joseph Mohr**

Beloved People of Christ,

Once again, it is the holiest of evenings, Christmas Eve. I remember one very special Christmas Eve when I was an assistant priest at St. Nikolaus Church in Oberndorf in the Alps of Austria.

It was 1818. The church organ had broke down. Because of this, we needed a Christmas hymn which could be played on another instrument. A new hymn had to be written ... and I didn't have much time. Nevertheless, I managed to write a six-verse Christmas carol. On December 24, I gave it to the church organist and teacher in the village school, Franz Gruber. He set my words to music.

The two of us sang SILENT NIGHT, HOLY NIGHT! for the first time during the Christmas Eve midnight mass that night, he singing tenor, and I singing bass while I strummed on the guitar. The parish choir joined in repeating the last two lines in four-part harmony. I will never forget this humble scene.

The man who repaired the organ, Karl Mauracher from Zillerthal, took a copy of the song after repairing our organ. Although it wasn't published for twenty years, it was well known in Tyrol, a province in Austria. The carol was sung by touring families from the area. In 1833 I wrote an arrangement for choir, organ, and orchestra. Five years later, SILENT NIGHT, HOLY NIGHT! was published in a German hymnal.

An Episcopal Bishop in the United States, John Freeman Young, translated STILLE NACHT, HEILIGE NACHT! into English. It was published at first in 1863 and then in 1887. The bishop chose verses 1, 6, and 2 in that order.

Never did I think it would continue to be sung *every* Christmas Eve. SILENT NIGHT, HOLY NIGHT! is now a beloved carol. It seems to be the most loved of them all. Do you think it is because beauty shines in simplicity?

Like love found in a stable. Rejoice! Christ is born!

                                                                  Joseph Mohr
                                                                  (1792-1848)

Christmas Day   **Isaac Watts**

Dear Saints of Christ,

    What happiness dwells in my heart knowing that Christmas Day is here once more. Again, God has bestowed upon us the privilege of celebrating the birth of our Savior and His Son, Jesus, the Christ.

    You might say that I liked the idea of celebrating God's Word in song, for that was one of my many endeavors during my life. My father wanted to get us out of a musical rut, you might say. For at the time, the Church of England only allowed the singing of dull metrical psalms. Consequently, he challenged me to improve the *status quo* of English hymns, to write ones instead that resounded with praise! I took up the challenge.

    However, first I attended an academy at Stoke Newington. After completing my studies, I returned home. For the next two years I devoted myself to writing hymns. Many of them were published in *Hymns and Spiritual Songs*.

    By 1699, I was assistant at a dissenting church, Mark Lane, in London. Three years later, I was ordained. At this time, I also became minister there.

    As the year passed, I continued writing hymns. Altogether, I wrote approximately 600 of them. In 1712 my health began to suffer. From then on, I was forced to slow down, just as anyone does when he or she is overworked.

    I am known as the "Father of English Hymnody." But on this festival day we call Christmas, a far greater Gift was given by a far greater Father. Join the whole company of heaven and earth in singing my Christmas carol, JOY TO THE WORLD.

    Reecho the praise of the first Christmas!

                                                            Isaac Watts
                                                         (1674-1748)

Christmas 1 — James Montgomery

Dear People in Christ,

    I put my pen down as much as I could to celebrate the birth of Christ during the twelve days of Christmas.

    You see, I was always in literary circles although this was not the intention of my parents. My father was a Moravian minister. When I was a young boy, my parents sailed to the West Indies as missionaries while I remained home at a boarding school in England. It was Father's intention that I should be a minister also. I never saw my parents again. Both Mother and Father died in those faraway lands.

    I wasn't interested in school. Often I was caught writing poetry. At last I had to drop out. At first I worked in a bake shop, but then I ran away. It was hard to find a job as a youth on the streets. For a while I sold a poem for a guinea. Then, I worked in two clerking positions.

    At last I landed a job as a columnist in the *Sheffield Register,* which I later bought and renamed the *Sheffield Iris.* However, I wrote two controversial columns during this time and ended up in prison. This gave me extra time to continue writing more poetry. It was during my early years that I wrote most of my 400 hymns.

    I continued on in literary circles lecturing on poetry. Finally the British government gave me a literary pension of 200 pounds a year. In addition, I spoke up for the underprivileged and championed foreign missions.

    Only a poem, "Nativity," was to be found in my column on December 24, 1816. I was merely reprinting a birth announcement. The poem, which eventually became ANGELS, FROM THE REALMS OF GLORY, was five stanzas in length. However, I understand that today many hymnals contain only three with an added doxology by another person.

    Angels, God's messengers, made the greatest birth announcement in history.

Angels, from the realms of glory,
Wing your flight o'er all the earth;
Once you sang creation's story;
Now proclaim Messiah's birth:

Come and worship, come and worship,
Worship Christ, the newborn king.

James Montgomery
(1771-1854)

The Name of Jesus — John Newton

Dear Ones in the Name of Jesus, the Christ,

It was during my early years sailing for the Royal Navy as well as in my early years as a slave trader that I turned my back on God. Although my mother was a God-fearing woman, she died when I was but seven. When I was eleven, my father took me with him on the high seas.

From the Navy, I went into the slave trade. The slaves I brought back from Africa were nameless to me. While I was en route on one of my later voyages there was nothing to do. I picked up *Imitation of Christ* by Thomas à Kempis and started reading.

I began to reflect on my childhood religious training. A terrible storm occurred on this voyage. I prayed "like the cry of the ravens, which yet the Lord does not disdain to hear." That was in 1748, from which I date my "conversion experience." Six years later, I gave up the slave trade.

I married my sweetheart, Mary Catlett, in 1750. While preparing for the ministry, I held a position as tide surveyor. Although ordained a priest in the Church of England several years later, I was always amazed that God could forgive me. For I had been that former slave trader, a wretch.

When I was eighty years, my sight failed me, and an aide assisted me in my preaching at St. Mary's in London. One Sunday, he told me the first point of my sermon. I said to the worshipers, "Jesus Christ is precious." He said the next point. Again, I said, "Jesus Christ is precious." The aide thought I had made a mistake, but I said to him, "And I'll say it again, Jesus Christ is precious," after which I asked the congregation to sing my hymn, HOW SWEET THE NAME OF JESUS SOUNDS.

What's in the Name of Jesus? Everything.

John Newton
(1725-1807)

Epiphany Day

William Chatterton Dix

My Dear Friends in Christ,

It is good to be with you in spirit during the Season of Epiphany. Although I was manager of a marine insurance company in Glasgow, Scotland, I loved to write poetry. As an active Anglican layman, I especially liked to write religious poetry. Born to a surgeon in Bristol, I was named for the English poet Chatterton.

AS WITH GLADNESS MEN OF OLD was written when I was ill and could not attend an Epiphany service. As I lay there in bed, I read the Gospel for the day. I was inspired and began to reflect on the text. Taking a pen, I started putting my thoughts on paper. By evening, I was holding this hymn in my hand. I was in my early twenties at the time.

It didn't take long before AS WITH GLADNESS MEN OF OLD was published. The year following, 1859, it was included in the trial copy of the famous hymnal, *Hymns Ancient and Modern*. AS WITH GLADNESS MEN OF OLD then had the honor of being one of the hymns included in the *original edition* of this hymnal printed in 1861. It was included as well in my own collection, *Hymns of Love and Joy* of the same year.

In my position with the insurance company, I traveled a great deal, bringing gifts back from afar with me. The Wise Men, too, traveled from afar bringing unique and costly gifts. They found, just as I had, a far greater Gift. Their treasures had a price. But the Gift they found was priceless, beyond any amount of money imaginable.

Join the Wise Men. Be truly wise in discerning your treasured gifts.

William Chatterton Dix
(1837-1898)

Epiphany 1   **Christopher Wordsworth**

Dear People of Christ,

    We are in the Season of Epiphany or Christ's manifestations. Another way to put it is, this is the season when Christ reveals Himself as the Son of God. Praise Him for His acts in which He still reveals Himself to you, His saints on earth!

    I was a bit of a poet like my uncle William Wordsworth as well as following my father in his profession as a clergyman. Consequently, I was a priest in the Church of England, finally becoming a bishop.

    I especially liked to teach through that spark of artistic poetry which seemed to be ingrained in me. As a result, I put together a liturgical church hymnal based on the days and seasons of the Church titled *Holy Year: Hymns for Sundays, Holidays, and Other Occasions throughout the Year,* 1862.

    As you sing my hymn SONGS OF THANKFULNESS AND PRAISE, I mention *all* the manifestations in which Jesus reveals that He is indeed the Christ ... Please note the *first* manifestation, His baptism at the River Jordan.

    At His baptism, we read in Saint Matthew 3:17 His Father saying to Him, "This is my Son, the Beloved, with whom I am well pleased." The Holy Spirit also descends upon Jesus in the form of a dove. This act of baptism announces the beginning of His ministry on earth.

    Baptism. Have you thought about it? It marked the change from Christ's life as a carpenter to revealing Himself as the Son of God, the Messiah. Have you thought about your own baptism?

    If you wish to read more about baptism you may read a commentary on the Bible or look at the commentary on God's Word which I wrote. Baptism — putting on Christ.

    Telling the world that we belong to Him.

                                                         Christopher Wordsworth
                                                             (1807-1885)

Epiphany 2   **Frank Mason North**

Dear Friends in Christ,

I am amazed that my hymn WHERE CROSS THE CROWDED WAYS OF LIFE is still being sung. I did not think at the time when it was being written in 1903 that it would be popular so many years later!

You see, I never considered myself a *hymnwriter*. First and foremost, I considered myself to be a minister of our Lord serving the Methodist church. I had parishes in Florida, New York, and Connecticut. Then I came back to city of my birth in 1892.

Here in New York City, I served as editor of *The Christian City* for the next twenty years as well as being secretary of the Methodist Episcopal Church. WHERE CROSS THE CROWDED WAYS OF LIFE came into my mind as I was preparing a sermon on Matthew 22:9. It was first printed in *The Christian City* in 1903. Two years later, the hymn appeared in *The Methodist Hymnal*. I really never thought it would be printed in *other* hymnals, too! For I just didn't see myself as that *hymnwriter*!

What I did see in New York City was the great need for being a missionary right here where I was living ... where God put me. There were many who had not heard the "Good News"! For some, Wall Street was a god which consumed its followers. There were also the bruised and the broken who needed my ministry, the people society doesn't care about even though Our Lord and Savior does.

You don't have to go very far to be a missionary. And if you think you're not one, remember I didn't think I was that *hymnwriter* either! Be a missionary "at home," just as I embraced the missionary field of New York City. Minister to your neighbors who are homeless and without food. Can't you see the face of Jesus in their want and need? Can't you see the face of our suffering Savior in their faces? Embrace them all ...

With the love of Christ and His compassion.

                                                    Frank Mason North
                                                    (1850-1935)

Epiphany 3   **Elisabeth Cruciger**

My dear Sisters and Brothers in Christ,

Once again, the season of Light or Epiphany is here. It is a good time to contemplate the meaning of Christmas.

During my years on earth, I didn't have much time for reflection up until the Season of Epiphany. Christmas was a very busy time for us, as it is for you. Like you, I was kept occupied with many preparations for our family. What a privilege it always was to celebrate the Holy Day of Christmas and the days afterward.

We were a bustling little family. My husband, Casper, was often preaching with our dear brother, Martin Luther. He worked with Martin a good deal of the time. As Katie Luther was a friend of mine, sometimes I thought we lived at the Luther home!

Of course, Katie and I had been friends for years. We had much in common, being former nuns who married pastors. Martin always referred to my husband as his most promising pupil. How much they enjoyed each other's company!

Casper and I had two children, Casper and Elisabeth. They brought us much pleasure. Often they played with the Luther children. In fact, our daughter married one of the Luther sons.

My hymn, THE ONLY SON FROM HEAVEN, was printed in the second and third hymnals (Lutheran) which came out in 1524 soon after the Reformation had begun. These song books appeared in Erfurt and Wittenberg. What an honor it was to be the *first* published German woman hymnwriter. As this is a Christmas/Epiphany hymn, it was dear to my heart.

I pondered the meaning of Christmas and the Epiphany message of salvation for all through Christ, our Savior. I did this as I was writing THE ONLY SON FROM HEAVEN. Read or sing my first printed hymn. Ponder with me.

Won't you?

                                                                       Elisabeth Cruciger
                                                                          (1500-1535)

Epiphany 4   **William Arthur Dunkerley**

Dear People in Christ,

    Wherever you are, I would like to encourage you to share the Good News of the love of Christ, to all people. This time of Epiphany is an especially good time to tell of His great love for everyone!
    Like the Wise Men, I was "on the go." After finishing my schooling at the University of Manchester, I served the French side in my father's business. He was a wholesale merchant. Five years later, I married a woman from Scotland. From there we went to the United States, where I opened a division of the family business. I also did some writing in *The Detroit Free Press*.
    Returning to England, I had my own newspaper. From then on I was an established journalist. My writing met with great success. During my life I wrote over twenty books of poetry and prose in addition to forty novels. However, I had several names for my writing, like "John Oxenham" or at other times "Julian Ross." Some of my best friends never knew all three names belonged to me!
    Active in the Congregational Church, I included IN CHRIST THERE IS NO EAST OR WEST in *The Pageant of Light and Darkness*. This pageant was part of the London Missionary Exhibition held in London in 1905. The pageant, which I also wrote, was the biggest attraction of the exhibition. IN CHRIST THERE IS NO EAST OR WEST was published eight years later in my book *Bees of Amber*.
    In my travels, I had met many people from many countries. I knew Christ loved them all.
    Jesus is *everyone's* Savior.

    Join hands then, brothers of the faith,
    Whate'er your race may be.

                                        William Arthur Dunkerley
                                                    (1852-1941)

Epiphany 5 — Mary Ann Thomson

Dear Members of the Body of Christ,

Has something ever happened to make you sit down and write at that *very* moment? A note, a message, a letter right then and there?

Coming from England, I married John Thomson. He was the first librarian of the Free Library in Philadelphia. I belonged to the Church of the Annunciation. My husband was an account warden there. The Lord blessed our marriage with children.

The urge to write right then and there once happened to me on a night in 1868. I was only in my thirties at the time. One of our children came down with typhoid fever. Just a raging case. There our dear child lay. I could not leave the room. When I was sitting there, it suddenly came to me what was really important in life.

I began thinking of David Livingston. He was now lost in Africa. Why was he there? Livingston, of course, was there as a missionary. I knew the most important thing at that moment was that other people should know that eternal life comes through Jesus Christ.

I desperately wanted my child to live. I prayed. In my heart, I wanted this child someday to follow in Livingtson's steps. To be a missionary. But my child was still a child and lay gravely ill.

I picked up my pen while staying in the room and began writing O ZION, HASTE. I had always wanted to write a missionary text for a hymn tune of which I was particularly fond.

I added the refrain around three years later. O ZION, HASTE is one of approximately forty hymns which I wrote. It was published in the *Church Hymnal* of 1892 (Episcopal) to the tune with which it became associated.

However, back on that night back in 1868, I realized what was important. Telling the world about our loving Savior seemed to me to be one the most important tasks in life.

Is it one of yours?

Mary Ann Thomson
(1834-1923)

Epiphany 6 — Johann Heermann

My dear Ones in Christ, our Savior,

    I was one of five children born to a poor furrier and his wife. As it turned out, I was the only one that survived, athough I, too, was very ill. My mother promised God that I would serve Him as a Lutheran pastor if I were allowed to live. Like Hannah, she dedicated me to the Lord ... and it was an honor to be His servant.

    I served in only one place, Koben, Germany. By 1616, the town was reduced to ashes by a devastating fire. The next year my dear wife died, and the year after that the Thirty Years' War began. You might say that from 1616, life grew difficult for me.

    Koben was the scene of intense fighting. It was plundered four times. Each time I fled and was robbed of my possessions. Four times I had to start all over again. Once when fleeing, I was shot at several times. In 1631, the pestilence came to Koben. Now we had not only war, but also illness. The only one to turn to was Christ Himself.

    I would have given up, given in to despair. But rather than doing this, I groped through the darkness of war looking for light from Heaven. In O CHRIST, OUR LIGHT, O RADIANCE TRUE, I prayed for *all* to come to the knowledge of our Savior. I prayed for God's grace. One of my 400 hymns, it was printed in 1630 in my *Devoti Musica Cordis* under the section, "In the time of the persecution and distress of pious Christians."

    My life was somewhat like those of Paul Gerhardt and Martin Rinckart. We spread God's Word in times of utter devastation. Fools for Christ. By the world's standards, we were all "losers" having nothing.

    Or were we?

Johann Heermann
(1585-1647)

Transfiguration Sunday   **Joseph Robinson**

Dear People in Christ,

    Today is the culmination of the Season of Epiphany before we descend into the valley of Lent. This is the day which the Church calls Transfiguration Day. The Gospel reading shows us a glimpse of Christ in utter splendor with Moses and Elijah. Oh! How the two of them wished to stay on that mountaintop with Jesus forever.

    In commemoration of this event, I wrote the hymn HOW GOOD, LORD, TO BE HERE! It tells the story of this particular event in a straightforward, simple style quite opposite to the life I led. It seemed like I was forever moving around involved with the Church of England. I served in many capacities ... an assistant curate, a professor of divinity, as well as once being a dean and a canon.

    HOW GOOD, LORD, TO BE HERE! was first published in the 1904 copy of the classic hymnal, *Hymns Ancient and Modern*. It is usually sung to a classic tune as well, one by the great J. S. Bach. Mind you, it was never composed as a tune for any hymn. The tune *Potsdam* comes from the second fugue in E major found in Bach's *Forty-eight Preludes and Fugues*.

    As for the name *Potsdam*, it refers to the famous visit paid by Bach to King Frederick "the Great" of Prussia in 1747. Frederick was living in Potsdam outside of Berlin. During Bach's visit, Frederick had him test various organs in the city as well as his new Silbermann pianoforte at the palace. Upon his return to Leipzig, Bach wrote his *Musical Offering* for the king. The visit was a scene of grand splendor.

    But I tell you, there was more glory to behold on that mountaintop when Christ appeared dressed in a white garment. The Church, in her wisdom, remembers this event. For the whole countenance of Jesus radiated with dazzling splendor.

    More splendor than the palace of a king.

                                            Joseph Robinson
                                               (1858-1933)

Ash Wednesday   **Nikolaus Decius**

Dear Friends of Christ,

I always seemed to wander. Here is part of my fragmented story.

After receiving part of my education, I went to a cloister. From there in 1515, I went to Braunschweig in northern Germany. There I was a teacher. It was while living in Braunschweig that I learned Low German. Getting restless after four years, I left to be prior of a nunnery near Wolfenbuettel.

When prior there, I became quite interested in what Martin Luther had to say. Once again, I wandered. After several short stints, I returned to Braunschweig. By this time, the city had embraced the Reformation.

Braunschweig then became the perfect place for me to circulate parts of the liturgy in Low German. I did this in a book I published in 1523 called *Summula*. This book also contained selections from the Gospel of Saint Matthew, works of Latin authors, and poetry in Low German.

The parts of the liturgy that I translated into this dialect were the *Gloria in Excelsis (Glory to God), Sanctus (Holy, Holy, Holy),* and *Agnus Dei (O Lamb of God)*. In addition, I adapted tunes for them from other sources, composing their melodies as well.

All three sections which I translated eventually became hymns in their own right. All three of them were published in Low German in 1531 and in High German in 1539. *The Agnus Dei*, O LAMB OF GOD, PURE AND SINLESS, is often used during Lent.

My spirit was restless. During the next several years I wandered. The last anyone had heard, I was in Muehlhausen. Here were Calvinists of Dutch origin. I had great empathy for them.

As their community was expanding, I was moving on to another place once more. No one has heard or seen me since that time in 1546. Although I continued to roam, I never wandered away from Christ.

We are never out of His sight.

Nikolaus Decius
(1485-*)

*After 1546, the life of Nikolaus Decius is unknown.

Lent 1   **Martin Luther**

Dear People in Christ,

I am writing you this letter to urge you to keep singing God's holy Word. Sing the hymns of the Church in joy and in sorrow. They will give you strength to face whatever occurs in life. Even death itself.

In addition to translating the Bible, I wrote many hymns. I thought we should all sing the Gospel's message. I believe my most famous one is A MIGHTY FORTRESS IS OUR GOD. You might say it was the "Hymn of the Reformation."

As you will remember, I married my Katie, Katherine von Bora, in 1525. Our marriage was blessed with six beautiful children whom we loved dearly.

I faced many trials in my life. However, there was no trial as great as when our daughters, Elisabeth and Magdalena, died. I would have never survived this near all-encompassing grief if I could not have turned to God in prayer as well as in music — the Gospel in hymns.

No one more dear was ever taken from me than our two daughters. Oh, our precious infant, Elisabeth! As for Magdalena, she died in my arms. Magdalena had been such an obedient child. I never had to reprove her in her thirteen years.

When my friends tried to comfort me at the time of Magdalena's death, all I could say was, "I have sent a saint, a living saint, to Heaven." Katie took Magdalena's death especially hard. *I* had to console Katie. All we could do was to sing away our despair. Together, Katie and I sang our hearts out to the Lord.

I encourage you to keep in tune with the Gospel, with its message that Christ died for all ... including our precious daughters. For your loved ones, as well as for you and for me, God *is* a mighty fortress, indeed!

Martin Luther
(1483-1546)

Lent 2   **Thomas Kingo**

Dear Friends in Christ,

I am known as the first great hymnwriter of Denmark. However, I would have never guessed that this honor would be bestowed upon me. I had many difficulties with the hymns I wrote. The King of Denmark was "on my case," so to speak.

After I finished my early schooling, I attended the University of Copenhagen, where I completed my theological studies. After being a tutor for a short time, at last I was a parish pastor. I served several churches. Then I was consecrated a Lutheran bishop in 1677 as well as becoming a member of Denmark's nobility two years later.

I not only had parishes, but our many, many children! Officially they were my stepchildren. You see, I married two widows with large families. The children were always coming ... and going.

After the death of my second wife, I married a young noblewoman. We had a very happy marriage without any children. My third wife insisted on coming with me on all my pastoral visits.

During the years, I wrote many hymns. In 1683, the King of Denmark appointed me to prepare a new hymnal. This was published in 1689. However, the King of Denmark did not like this songbook. Someone else was appointed, but the hymnal which appeared four years later did not please the King either. A committee, as usual, was struck for this Danish hymnal. This one *was* published in 1699. This new hymnal contained 85 of my hymns.

ON MY HEART IMPRINT YOUR IMAGE was in the hymnal of 1689 which I prepared. This hymn of mine was originally a long one on the crucifixion of Christ. The hymn as you know it today is only the fifteenth verse. Because the hymn now begins with a different verse, it is known by a new name. ON MY HEART IMPRINT YOUR IMAGE is a beautiful title, isn't it?

Beautiful enough to have engraved on our hearts forever.

                                                                      Thomas Kingo
                                                                       (1634-1703)

Lent 3   Nicolaus Ludwig von Zinzendorf

Dear Sisters and Brothers in Christ,

I was born into German nobility in Dresden, Germany. By the age of nineteen, I received a degree from Wittenberg University. From there, I accepted a government position in my native city and married.

Three years later, the Moravian Brethren approached me for a place to settle as they were being persecuted. I offered them the use of one of my estates. The Moravians named it "Herrnhut." It became a haven for persecuted Christians fleeing Bohemia and Moravia.

I became interested in the teachings of the Moravians. At the end of five years, I joined them. In 1734, I was licensed to preach by the University of Tuebingen. Several years later, I was consecrated a bishop.

However, I had opponents. These opponents were successful in obtaining an edict which banished me from the area for the next ten years.

I used this opportunity to do mission work. In those years, I traveled to many countries in Europe as well as going to America and the West Indies. After the edict was lifted, I returned to "Herrnhut," which became the new Moravian headquarters for missions. I remained there for the rest of my life.

Throughout all those busy years, I wrote approximately 2,000 hymns. I began writing them at the age of twelve and never put down my pen until just days before I died.

Wherever I was, I always remembered that Jesus died for me. While returning from the West Indies in 1739, I wrote JESUS, YOUR BLOOD AND RIGHTEOUSNESS. Originally it had 33 stanzas. I never ceased to marvel that Christ remembered me when He died on Calvary. Christ remembered you, too, when He shed His precious blood on the Cross.

Have you remembered Him?

Nicolaus Ludwig von Zinzendorf
(1700-1760)

Lent 4   **Elizabeth Cecelia Clephane**

Dear Ones in Christ,

I spent my whole life in Scotland. My father was sheriff in the area of Edinburgh. After Father died, I left with my two sisters for other parts of the country. At first we went to Ormiston, East Lothian.

From there we traveled to Bridgend in Melrose. Here you can see the bridge to which Sir Walter Scott refers in *Abbott and the Monastery*. After settling in Melrose, my sisters and I made it our home for the rest of our lives.

During our stay there, we devoted our lives to charity. We enjoyed expressing the Christian faith we had in common between us by acts of love. Although my health was poor, I was determined to help others less fortunate in the community. History has dubbed me "The Sunbeam of Melrose" because of my cheerful attitude.

Our church was the Free Church of Scotland. I was fond of church and occasionally penned a hymn. Although I liked church, I loved Christ and His Cross even more, for I could take them with me when the church service ended. I wrote this in BENEATH THE CROSS OF JESUS.

I took Christ and His Cross with me when I was helping others. He gave me the strength to go on and continue in my acts of charity. I found the Cross like "a mighty rock," "a home within a wilderness," as well as a resting place "upon the way."

In my mind's eye, I could see Jesus suffering there for the whole world. That brought to mind both my sin and His great redeeming love for me as well. When suffering, He loved you dearly even at this moment in time.

I could take Jesus and His Cross anywhere I went, in any situation. When I was but 38, Jesus and His Cross were there for me as I went to my eternal rest. I knew I could depend on Christ and His Cross all my life.

And in my hour of death.

                                                     Elizabeth Cecelia Clephane
                                                                 (1830-1869)

Lent 5   **Erdmann Neumeister**

Dear People of Christ,

   For most of my life, I was pastor at St. James in Hamburg, Germany. I served this Lutheran parish for over forty years. While I loved to preach, I liked to write. I wrote over 650 hymns.
   I am also remembered for my concern regarding worship. Why this God of ours ... He deserved so much honor, so much praise! Who was I in the presence of God, the Perfect One? Just like the rest of you, I was a poor sinner who stood in need of forgiveness.
   And therein lay the eternal mystery. That Jesus, the Sinless One, should die for me. As a human being, I had inherited the condition of sin, just as we all did from our first parents, Adam and Eve.
   The issue at hand was nothing less than *sin and grace.* Grace that Christ would keep company with me, a sinner. Grace that He should keep company with you sinners, although I understand the word *sin* is not in vogue at this present time.
   I was awed by the mystery. So struck by the fact that Jesus would keep company with me that I wrote JESUS SINNERS WILL RECEIVE.
   However, I was not the only one who was awed by the presence of Jesus Christ with sinners. There was a very famous composer who felt this way, too. His name was Johann Sebastian Bach or the "Fifth Evangelist," as Albert Schweitzer later called him. Bach wanted to get the same message out to the Church and to the world through his music.
   The "Fifth Evangelist" felt this so intensely about *sin and grace* that the majority of his works are religious. In addition to writing hymns, I also penned many of the texts of Bach's now well-known cantatas which express the forgiveness of Christ.
   Bach is still getting the message of *sin and grace* out, for I understand his musical works are still being sung around the world

today. Jesus is still patiently waiting to receive all who ask for forgiveness.

Are you asking?

Erdmann Neumeister
(1671-1756)

Palm Sunday   **Henry Milman**

Dear Followers of Christ,

My father was a physician in the Court of England. He was one of several doctors to King George III, whom you may remember battled with the American colonies in the Revolutionary War.

However, I did not wish to follow in father's footsteps. I wanted to serve a far greater King. My talent was poetry, prose, and Latin verse. I took it all with me after receiving a master's degree when I became a priest in the Church of England in 1816.

However, after five years, I was back at the university, this time as professor of poetry at Oxford. From there I lectured at Brampton. Serving in many other capacities *back* in the Church, my last position was as dean of St. Paul's Cathedral in London.

I contributed thirteen hymns to a hymnal that my friend, Bishop Heber, had put together, *Hymns Written and Adapted to the Weekly Church Services of the Year.* Published in 1827, RIDE ON, RIDE ON IN MAJESTY was one of them.

Many years later, it was given a new tune. The composer was Graham George, an organist in the Episcopal Church in the United States. He tells us that it came into his head one morning after a choir practice. He had been practicing with the choir for the next Sunday, Palm Sunday. The first part of the tune came to him while having toast and marmalade at breakfast. Getting up, George went to his piano and the rest came to him. The tune is *King's Majesty.*

"Majesty." There is something just majestic in the word itself. On that first Palm Sunday, Jesus rode into the city of Jerusalem as a Majesty. The people hailed Him as one. But in just five days that same crowd turned on Him. They missed the "Majesty" right before their eyes.

Do you see His Majesty?

                                                                  Henry Milman
                                                                  (1791-1868)

Maundy Thursday   **Johann Rist**

Dear Members of the Body of Christ,

Unlike most pastors, I only served in one parish, which was in Wedel near Hamburg, Germany. The Lord entrusted me with both the spiritual as well as the physical health of the inhabitants in Wedel and the surrounding area.

For I was a pastor as well as a physician. This was my only church, although I could have had positions elsewhere. However, I decided to remain with my faithful flock, where I spent more than thirty years. I was only 28 when I settled here. To Wedel, I brought my bride, Elisabeth Stapfel.

In addition to being both a clergyman and physician, I also loved to write hymns. Approximately 680 flowed from my pen on every aspect of theology. I learned to write them on the "impulse of the moment." I was taught this technique at the university in Rinteln by the hymnwriter, Josua Stegmann.

My hymns were sung all over Germany while I was at Wedel. They were sung in both the Lutheran and Roman Catholic churches. However, one Lutheran church did not sing them. Which one? You probably guessed Wedel. If you did, you're right! As the old saying goes, a person is never honored in his hometown. However, that did not matter. Everyone else was singing them!

O LIVING BREAD FROM HEAVEN I wrote for Holy Communion which in my time was celebrated often. The bread I handed out as a pastor was far different from the bread we all ate around the tables in our homes. For it was not only *life-giving*, but *living*! And we used one cup, the chalice, representing our unity as the communion of saints.

I attended five universities and was crowned *poet laureate* by the Emperor. While these are blessings, I was concerned in matters of the heart, just like the beloved physician, Saint Luke. You might say Saint Luke and I had much in common.

Even though 1600 years had come and gone.

                                                        Johann Rist
                                                       (1607-1667)

Good Friday   **Cecil Frances Humphreys Alexander**

Dear Children of Christ,

    As a minister's wife in Londonderry, Ireland, I walked many miles caring for the poor and needy My husband, the Reverend William Alexander, remarked, "From one poor home to another she went. Christ was ever with her, and in her, and all felt her influence." I must admit I felt His abiding presence.

    I have always had a special place in my heart for you, the children. Countless times when I was visiting or had you in Sunday school, I would talk about the Bible, the Creed, and the catechism. Attempting to explain the doctrines of the Church, I wrote hymns just for you. The result ... most of my songs are for children.

    In response to the part of the Apostles' Creed, "suffered under Pontius Pilate, was crucified, dead, and buried," I penned THERE IS A GREEN HILL FAR AWAY. I wrote this hymn while visiting a child who was sick in bed.

    As for myself, I was born in Ireland. By the age of nine, I was already writing poetry. Since Father served as an officer of the Royal Marines and was rather strict, I was not sure that he would like my poems. Consequently, I stashed my poetry under a carpet! However, when Father discovered this, he spent an hour together with me every Saturday night. During this "quality time," as you call it, he read my poems out loud.

    Out of my love for you children, as well as expressing the teachings of the Church, came what some have called my most famous work. *Hymns for Little Children* was published in 1848. The profits of this book went towards children who were "challenged" in life. This hymnbook was published in over 100 editions.

    All together, I wrote approximately 400 hymns and poems. Although most of my hymns are for children, *all of God's children* can identify with THERE IS A GREEN HILL FAR AWAY.

    For in dying on the Cross, Jesus *loved us all.*

                        Cecil Frances Humphreys Alexander
                              (1818/1823?-1895)

Easter Sunday   **Christian Fuerchtegott Gellert**

Dear Friends in Christ on this joyous Easter Day,

    I spent my life rejoicing in this fact that Jesus lives! I wrote my hymns in a period of Church history when Rationalism started appearing on the scene. This meant that reason over faith prevailed in the Church. However, I was not interested in this new "age."

    In choosing a career, I followed in my father's profession, choosing the Lutheran ministry. Starting out I was assistant to my father. However, when it came to preaching, I just could not remember the whole content of the sermon.

    You realize, of course, that we pastors were not allowed to have manuscripts of our sermons with us in the pulpit. That was forbidden. As my memory often failed me when there, I gave up the idea of the ministry. However, that didn't dampen my faith. I just realized that my "calling" lay elsewhere. My first position after this was as a private tutor.

    My career "took off," you might say, after I received my Master of Arts degree. For I took my Christian faith into the philosophy department where I was a lecturer. Taking an interest in my students, they in turn liked my lectures for both their style and their content.

    Among the students I taught were Johann Wolfgang von Goethe as well as Gotthold Ephraim Lessing. Both became distinguished literary figures in Germany. Because of my wit and humor, I won a place of esteem among the German classicists. By 1751, I was assistant professor of philosophy. Finally I was offered a full professorship, but I refused because of failing health.

    Perhaps God wanted me in the philosophy department all along. For here I confronted students who embraced Rationalism. While I enjoyed teaching philosophy, it was not my god. My faith shines in the 54 hymns I wrote. JESUS LIVES! THE VICTORY'S WON! is my confession of our Easter faith. My ultimate confidence lay in Christ and His Resurrection.

Easter confidence. A gift divine.

Jesus lives! The vict'ry's won!
Death no longer can appall me;
Jesus lives! Death's reign is done!
From the grave will Christ recall me.
Brighter scenes will then commence;
This shall be my confidence.

Christian Fuerchtegott Gellert
(1715-1769)

Easter 2   **Samuel Medley**

Dear Saints in Christ,

In I KNOW THAT MY REDEEMER LIVES! I repeated the phrase "He lives" over and over again. I often did this with many of the hymns which I wrote. This particular phrase can never be said too many times!

I started out in life as an apprentice to an oilman in London. Disliking it, I quit and joined the Royal Navy. When at Port Lagos, I suffered a severe wound to my leg. I was only in my early twenties. This physically impaired me for the rest of my life. Consequently, I was forced to leave the Navy.

I then went to live with my devout grandfather. During my stay, he read me a sermon by Isaac Watts. I was deeply moved upon hearing its message. Because of this experience, I joined the Baptist Church on Eagle Street. The famous preacher, George Whitefield, often preached there.

I married in 1762 and went to Soho. Here I established a school. Four years later, I began to preach. The following year, I was a pastor at the Baptist Church in Watford, Hertfordshire.

From there, I moved on to a congregation in Liverpool in 1772. I remained there for the next 27 years. Due to my short career in the Navy, many of the seafaring population could identify with me. And I with them. The congregation grew.

Finally, a new meeting house had to be built. It was while I was in Liverpool that I KNOW THAT MY REDEEMER LIVES! was published. It appeared in George Whitefield's *Psalms and Hymns* of 1775, the 21st edition.

Today is the first Sunday after Easter. At last, Thomas joined the disciples. He joined them, saying with astonishment, "He lives." From then on, Thomas repeated the phrase over and over. In fact, he could never repeat it *enough*!

Are you repeating "He lives"? With Thomas and with me?

                                                        Samuel Medley
                                                         (1738-1799)

Easter 3   Birgitte Katerine Boye

Dear People in Christ,

It is my hope that you are singing my hymn HE IS ARISEN! GLORIOUS WORD! during this festival season of Easter! It is only one stanza in length. This long stanza is to be sung before the Gospel is read from Easter until Ascension Day announcing the Easter Message.

I was born in Bentofte, Denmark. In my early twenties, I married Herman Hertz. At the time we were married, Herman was a forester.

I led a busy life just like many of you. God blessed our marriage with four children. However, on the side, I learned German, French, and English. I did this to read poetry in its original language and to translate the hymns of the Church.

In 1773, the *Society of the Advancement of the Liberal Arts* asked for contributions of sacred poetry. I provided the society with twenty hymns. Later, eighteen were chosen for a hymnal prepared by Lutheran Bishop Ludvig Harboe as well as the state secretary, Ove Guldberg.

Life had been going smoothly. But then, as so many of you know, circumstances changed overnight. Suddenly, my husband's job was gone. Like a pink slip. I approached Mr. Guldberg on the matter of finances. He, in turn, mentioned it to Prince Fredrik. As a result, our two sons were educated by the Prince himself.

Our situation grew even worse. My husband died. Prince Fredrik supported my family now. After three years, I remarried a man from the customshouse, Hans Boye.

During this time, I continued my literary interests. A hymnal was being prepared by the Bishop and Mr. Guldberg. When the *Psalmebog* came out in 1778, it contained 124 of my hymns and 24 of my translations. In addition, I wrote secular poetry as well as drama which was often performed at the royal court.

I outlived my second husband as well. However, God blessed me throughout my life. He was ever with me. No matter what was happening, I always clung to the words of the Easter Message.

Do you?

> *He is arisen! Glorious Word!*
> *Now reconciled is God, my Lord;*
> *The gates of heav'n are open.*
> *My Jesus rose triumphantly,*
> *And Satan's arrows broken lie,*
> *Destroyed hell's fiercest weapon.*
> *Oh, hear, what cheer!*
> *Christ victorious,*
> *Rising glorious,*
> *Life is giving.*
> *He was dead,*
> *but now is living!*

Birgitte Katerine Boye
(1742-1824)

Easter 4 — Henry W. Baker

My dear Friends in Christ,

When was the last time you saw gently rolling pastures with a meandering stream in the scene? Did you want to stay and behold this pastoral view ... not wanting to leave? I sketched that scene in my memory. For it was a place to pause and refresh oneself along life's busy way.

Born in London, I received two degrees from Trinity College at Cambridge. Ordained in 1844, I accepted the position as vicar in Monkland in Herefordshire. A "high church" Anglican, I believed that minsters should not marry. As a result, I had time to devote to "extra" projects.

The biggest one on which I worked was putting together a new hymnal for the Anglican Church. In fact, I was the chairman of the committee for twenty years. Compiling the hymnal, *Hymns Ancient and Modern,* was quite a task, I tell you.

People from all walks of life submitted their hymns. I had "free reign" as the editor to make changes. At least one person withdrew a hymn after I had edited it. In regard to this particular hymn, the author said the hymnal should be called *Hymns Asked For and Mutilated.* However, I did not let criticism bother me. I continued editing.

Finally in 1861, *Hymns Ancient and Modern* was published. By the time 1912 arrived, over sixty million copies had been sold. Quite a number! I would have never guessed *that* many copies would have been printed. Because this hymnal was so well-liked, many have applauded my efforts in editing and my contribution to hymnody.

Hymns Ancient and Modern was appended with one of my own hymns, THE KING OF LOVE MY SHEPHERD IS. You know, I just never forgot that pastoral scene, the refreshing view which also included our Good Shepherd. I understand that my paraphrase of Psalm 23 is still being sung today. I never forgot those words I wrote, either.

Perverse and foolish oft I strayed,
But yet in love he sought me,
And on his shoulder gently laid,
And home, rejoicing, brought me.

At the end, they were *my* last words.

Henry W. Baker
(1821-1877)

Easter 5   John Macleod Campbell Crum

Dear People of Christ,

We have been celebrating the resurrection of Christ now for many weeks during this joyous Easter Season.

By now, wherever you live in the northern hemisphere, you should be noticing a resurrection of the whole earth as well, whether you live on Vancouver Island in British Columbia, Canada, the prairies of the United States, or my native England.

Things outside should be "greening up." Even if you have the occasional snowstorm, the grass underneath *is* green. Flowers are beginning to bloom, from the small purple crocus found in the Province of Manitoba to the profusion of spring flowers in my country.

You might say the whole creation is alive again, just like our Lord. In looking outside, you see that green blade of grass, the sign of coming life. I wrote about the Risen Christ and the new life found in creation in NOW THE GREEN BLADE RISES.

I was asked to write this for a very special tune, *Noel Nouvelet.* The famous composer, Marcel Dupré, based his *Variations on a Noel* on this melody. It is a French carol. Putting my text with the tune, you have NOW THE GREEN BLADE RISES! My Easter carol first appeared in the *Oxford Book of Carols* printed in London in 1928.

As for myself, I was an Anglican clergyman. While faithful in serving many flocks at many churches throughout England, I always pursued an interest in writing. My last posts in the ministry were as canon of Canterbury and then canon emeritus of Canterbury.

Life is coming back. That's what it's all about. From the Cross on Good Friday to the Risen Christ on Easter. From the dead of Winter to the life of Spring.

Celebrate His resurrection. Sing my Easter carol!

                             John Macleod Campbell Crum
                                       (1872-1958)

Easter 6   **Ulrik Vilhelm Koren**

Dear People in Christ,

Sing with joy this Easter Season. Alleluia! Christ is risen! Sing with all your heart that Christ has conquered the grave!

I had a most interesting life ... all the way from a cathedral school in Bergen, Norway, to the prairies of the United States. After finishing my schooling at the University of Christiania in 1844, I taught school in my native community.

Following this short career, I was called to a parish all the way in Iowa. Ordained into the Church in 1853, I came with my wife, Else Elisabeth, to what is now Washington Prairie. I assumed my pastoral duties in December of that year.

Our first Christmas on the prairies. It was quite a change, I tell you! Probably one you can't even imagine! Here we made our home for the rest of our lives. I was the first Norwegian Lutheran pastor to serve a parish west of the Mississippi River.

During this time, I became active in the Norwegian Synod. First I became secretary. Later, I served as vice-president. For twenty years, 1874-1894, I further served as president of the Iowa District. In 1894, I became president of the Norwegian Lutheran Synod of America until 1910.

Involved in community affairs, I also helped many causes. Among them, I was active in establishing the Grieg Singing Society, the first mail route to go out of Decorah, and the Norwegian Mutual Insurance Company!

While serving both the synod and the community, I was always faithful to my flock in Washington Prairie near Decorah. By 1903, I preached my fiftieth Christmas sermon.

I was always interested in music and hymns of the Church. Because of my great love for both I was influential in having the *Rythmisk Koralbog* published. It contained 27 original hymns of mine as well as 21 that I had translated.

My hymn, OH! SING JUBILEE TO THE LORD, was published in the English hymnal, *The Lutheran Hymnary,* printed in

1913. Praising the Lord in song. I could never do it enough on my earthly pilgrimage.
   Can you?

Ulrik Vilhelm Koren
(1826-1910)

Ascension Day   **Thomas Kelly**

Dear People of Christ on this glorious day!

What a festive day is ours! For we celebrate the Ascension of Christ into Heaven. Jesus came to earth born in a lowly stall. He began His earthly ministry when He was baptized at the River Jordan. Three years later, the crowd crucified Him. In three days He rose, victorious. Now He has ascended to Heaven in kingly robes, leaving His grave clothes behind.

I wrote over 750 hymns in all. LOOK, THE SIGHT IS GLORIOUS is one of my finest, or so history has said. Ascension Day is very special. Very splendid. The Christian Church mentions it every time the Creed is said. Never let anyone tell you otherwise, for Christ is now reigning as King of kings!

I was born in Ireland, the son of a judge. I decided to study law also, receiving my education from Trinity College, Dublin. However, after reading and reflecting, I entered the ministry of the Church of Ireland (Anglican).

However, I soon went independent. This posed a problem for me as I didn't have a place in which to preach other than "just" buildings. And my preaching attracted many.

This problem was solved though when my wife and I put together our wealth. We used a portion of it to build chapels throughout Ireland where I could preach in "a house of God."

I also was known for being a friend of the poor and needy. During the terrible of famine of 1845-1849, God used me to feed the hungry. It was just my nature to work for the Lord *all* the time. For sixty years, I proclaimed the Gospel throughout Ireland. Eagerly, I preached the Good News of saving faith through Jesus our Savior.

As far as hymns are concerned, some have said I am to Ireland what Isaac Watts was to England. Do you get the picture?

But more importantly, do you get the picture of that first Ascension Day sight?

                                           Thomas Kelly
                                           (1769-1855)

Easter 7   **Frances Ridley Havergal**

Dear Friends in Christ,

What a joy it is to write this letter to you. Some people have referred to me as "a burst of sunshine" when I entered a room. I loved life and cherished being with people ... family, friends, acquaintances. Just everyone!

My father, an Anglican clergyman, called me "Quicksilver," as I was very fond of learning and learned very quickly! However, you will want to call me Frances, I'm sure. I was the youngest in our family.

I liked writing so very much that my first verses were published in *Good Words*, a religious periodical. I was only seven years of age at the time. As the years passed, I studied privately because of poor health. I was schooled both in England and in Germany.

During those years, I acquired a knowledge of French, German, Latin, Greek, and Hebrew. Having been blessed with a wonderful memory, I also memorized the complete New Testament as well as the Psalms.

I always felt my main calling in life was to tell everyone about the love of Jesus. An evangelist, you might say. I did this through missions and aid societies of the time. I communicated with people regardless of their walk in life. I read in servant's quarters and wrote letters to others and taught the Sunday school children. In addition, I did philanthropic work.

But for everyone, I wrote hymns. Writing them gave me constant pleasure. While holidaying in Wales in 1879, I died at the age of 42. Afterward, my sister gathered all of my hymns together. They were finally published in one volume. *Poetical Works* was printed in 1884.

O SAVIOR, PRECIOUS SAVIOR came out in 1874 in *Under the Surface*. It was listed beneath the heading "Christ Worshiped by the Church."

Today is the Sunday between Ascension and Pentecost. Christ had, by this time, ascended into Heaven.

O Savior, precious Savior, Whom yet unseen we love.

Although He is yet "unseen" to you, I know you love Him. Just as I do.

Frances Ridley Havergal
(1836-1879)

Pentecost   **Timothy Rees**

In the Spirit of Christ,

    Rejoice! This day the Church calls Pentecost is a day of celebration. For although Christ is not physically present with you on earth, the Comforter has come. The Holy Spirit has been dwelling with Christians since soon after Christ ascended into heaven. Since that day the Spirit of God has never left the Church.

    I faithfully served God's Church all my life. After taking my schooling in Wales and Scotland, I was ordained into the Church of England. I served in many ways such as curate, college chaplain, and lecturer.

    Later, I became a member of the Community of the Resurrection within the Anglican Church. In World War I, I was a chaplain, returning as principal of the College of the Resurrection. I also represented the Church in foreign missions. In the end, I held the office of bishop of Llandoff.

    When World War I was over, I was given a Military Cross for being chaplain. It was an honor I gained for serving my country. I could have never fulfilled my role as chaplain, however, were it not for God's Spirit.

    Having to face the wretched sights around me, I many times felt helpless trying to comfort the afflicted. I depended upon the Holy Spirit, the Comforter, for words when speaking to those in distress. In the hassle of an ugly war, the Comforter spoke grace-filled words through me.

    Yes, I received a Military Cross. But there was a Cross far greater. One that stood on Calvary holding the Savior of the world. And there was an honor far greater. One that I never deserved.

    The honor? That God should dwell in me. Just as He does in you. I wrote this in HOLY SPIRIT, EVER DWELLING. For God's Holy Spirit was ever with me even in my hour of deepest need, in the soldiers' hour of deepest need.

    In your hour of deepest need.

                                                          Timothy Rees
                                                          (1874-1939)

Trinity Sunday   **Reginald Heber**

Dear Saints in Christ,

I was a minister in the Church after completing my studies at Brasenose College, Oxford. I served for many years as vicar on the family estate in England. After this post, I was Bishop of Calcutta in faraway India. In this capacity, I had the privilege of ordaining the first native Anglican minister.

During my years in England, I saw much vice. On the other hand, in India, there was a vast sea of people who were in need of the Gospel.

I felt it was also my calling to improve the quality of hymns in the Anglican church. My superiors appreciated the many metrical psalms that were still being sung.

However, I wanted to weed still more of them out, giving us hymns that were grand and glorious to sing. In addition to the ones which came from own pen, I included those of others like Henry Milman in a new hymnal.

This hymnal was presented for use in our church in 1820. However, it did not get the stamp of approval for which I had hoped. Perhaps you have been in a similar situation. I must admit, I was disappointed.

I had contributed several hymns myself to this hymnal, which was the first of its kind in English. For it was organized according to the *Church Year*. The hymn Alfred Lord Tennyson thought was the best hymn ever written was one of mine, HOLY, HOLY, HOLY.

I was always in quest of the sacred, the spiritual. I wrote "Only Thou Art Holy." The tune to HOLY, HOLY, HOLY is *Nicaea*. It is named for the Council which met in 325 A.D. and formulated the doctrine of the Trinity in the Nicene Creed.

However, the hymnal eventually did gain acceptance. A role model for others which followed, *Hymns Written and Adapted to the Weekly Church Services of the Year* was published in both London and New York in 1827. It was one of a kind.

Like our God.

> *Holy, holy, holy,*
> *Lord God Almighty!*
> *Early in the morning*
> *our song shall rise to thee.*
> *Holy, holy, holy,*
> *merciful and mighty!*
> *God in three Persons,*
> *blessed Trinity!*

Reginald Heber
(1783-1826)

Pentecost 2   **Henry Lyte**

Dear Ones in Christ,

Rejoice and give praise to Christ. Now the King of Heaven! Where He reigns in glory as Lord. And His reign is without end. With time and space separating the earthly and heavenly Kingdoms, this concept is not always easy to grasp.

While on my earthly pilgrimage, I served God as a clergyman. As I seemed to have a gift for words, I was also a hymnwriter. Three volumes of my poetry were published while I was living.

A native of Scotland, I took my schooling at Trinity College in Dublin, Ireland. While at Trinity, I was awarded the prize for an English poem three different times. At first, I thought I wanted to study medicine. However, I decided I wanted to look after people's spiritual needs. Consequently, I chose the ministry and was ordained.

My first parish was at Taghmon, close to Wexford. From there I was transferred from one place to another. Perhaps you, too, know that feeling of constantly being moved around! Rather unsettling to say the least! At last, Lower Brixham, Devon, was "home." Here I served as curate for the remainder of my life.

PRAISE, MY SOUL, THE KING OF HEAVEN was published in my *Spirit of the Psalms* in 1834. The text is a paraphrase of a most beautiful psalm, Psalm 103.

The tune to which it is sung is called *Praise, My Soul,* which appeared in 1869. This royal tune was written by John Goss, the son of an organist.

Goss followed in his father's footsteps in addition to being a composer. When composing, he always asked for the Lord's blessing by putting the initials I.N.D.A., "In Nomine Domini. Amen," at the beginning of his music.

In his middle twenties, Goss became professor of harmony at the Royal Academy of Music. He held this position for the next 47 years. A decade later, he became organist at St. Paul's Cathedral in

London, a position he held until his retirement. Eventually, Goss was knighted by Queen Victoria.

I wrote my text for the finest of royalty, the King of Heaven. A regal tune adorns it.

In adoration of Christ, our Heavenly King.

> *Praise, my soul, the King of heaven;*
> *To his feet your tribute bring.*
> *Ransomed, healed, restored, forgiven,*
> *Evermore his praises sing.*
> *Alleluia! Alleluia!*
> *Praise the everlasting King!*
>
> *Angels help us to adore him,*
> *Who behold him face to face.*
> *Sun and moon bow down before him;*
> *All who dwell in time and space.*
> *Alleluia! Alleluia!*
> *Praise with us the God of grace.*

Henry Lyte
(1793-1847)

Pentecost 3   **Julie von Hausmann**

Dear Sisters and Brothers in Christ,

I was born into a Lutheran family living in Riga, Latvia, which was at that time a Russian Baltic province. Shortly after, our family moved to Mitau. My parents had seven daughters. Father taught to support the family. With Father teaching, education was a high priority in our home.

I studied with a private tutor. My migraine headaches often made studying difficult. If you have ever experienced a migraine headache, you'll know what I'm talking about. Although I understand great strides have been made in treating migraines, I also know that many of you still suffer from them.

By the time I was only in my early thirties, both my parents were in poor health. Mother died in 1859. Our family moved back to Riga two years later. I was very fond of Father. I looked after Father with loving care; he was blind. Often I caressed his large hands thinking of how he had led me. Finally, my father died.

While I was taking care of Father, my friend, Olga von Karp, saw my poetry. She gave it to Pastor Gustav Knak in Berlin. He liked what he read. He liked it so much that he asked for the whole collection, wanting to publish it.

I consented but with some stipulations. The conditions were that any benefit would go to a hospital and orphanage in Hong Kong. Furthermore, my name was not to be known. Four volumes in all, LORD, TAKE MY HAND AND LEAD ME was in the first volume published in 1862.

From Riga, I eventually went to St. Petersburg, Russia. Here my older sister, Elizabeth, was in charge of St. Anna School. The school was linked to a pension house. Here, four of us sisters worked and ministered to people ... spending many happy years together.

I lived my last years in Estonia. But no matter where I lived, I knew God's hand was always leading me.

Is God leading you, too?

                                                                        Julie von Hausmann
                                                                               (1825-1901)

Pentecost 4 — Maltbie Davenport Babcock

Dear Friends in Christ,

I was an athlete always on the go, you might say. But I also loved preaching God's Word and singing it.

Born in Syracuse, New York, I was educated at Syracuse University and Auburn Theological Seminary. Ordained into the ministry of the Presbyterian Church, my first parish was in Lockport, New York. The scenery in the surrounding area was nothing less than "pure delight."

As I had natural athletic abilities, I liked sports. I was a champion swimmer as well as a great baseball pitcher. And I loved to run. Athletics helped to keep me physically fit.

First Presbyterian in Lockport was close to Lake Ontario. Early in the morning I would tell my church staff, "I am going out to see my Father's world."

From the church I would run two miles to the top of a hill to see Lake Ontario. After seeing the lake, I would run another two miles to a deep ravine which was a haven for forty species of birds. I just loved to listen to their carols! Then, I ran four miles back to my church.

Liking music also, it should come as no surprise to anyone that I wrote THIS IS MY FATHER'S WORLD. I just had to tell you in a hymn about what I saw on my early morning run!

> *This is my Father's world;*
> *The birds their carols raise;*
> *The morning light, the lily white,*
> *Declare their maker's praise.*
> *This is my Father's world;*
> *He shines in all that's fair.*
> *In the rustling grass*
> *I hear him pass;*
> *He speaks to me ev'rywhere.*

Originally, this hymn had sixteen verses. THIS IS MY FATHER'S WORLD was published along with some of my other poetry and sermons in *Thoughts for Everyday Living*. This was printed in 1901 after I had departed this life.

It's amazing that the whole creation praises our Wondrous God, including the birds. Even if you can't run like I did, you can still hear the birds' carol.

And smell the roses.

Maltbie Davenport Babcock
(1858-1901)

Pentecost 5   **Charles Wesley**

Dear Servants of Christ's Church,

    I understand that you will be singing *one* of my 6,000 (!) hymns. It is rather hard to keep track of all these hymns, as you can well imagine! You know, a computer would have come in *very* handy.

    During the eighty years which God granted me, I was busy proclaiming His Word in sermons as well as in songs. However, I must admit that telling His story in music (as the text of a hymn) was God's gift to me. It was a joy rather than a chore to pen one hymn after another. The words came easily to me, just as your "God-given talent" comes easily to you. For each person has been blessed with a special gift.

    I traveled a good deal of my life. Graduating from Christ Church College, Oxford, I belonged to a group called the "Oxford Methodists" there. Several years later, I was ordained.

    Immediately, I left England as a missionary to Georgia. It wasn't long after that I became involved with Moravians. I traveled back to London to serve as curate, but once more I left. This time I joined my brother, John, as an itinerate preacher.

    Finally I returned to Bristol, where I served several Methodist Societies. Despite all of this, I still considered myself to be a lifelong member of the Anglican Church (although some could dispute this!).

    No matter where I served our Lord, I thought of myself as His servant proclaiming His wonderful Name. YOU SERVANTS OF GOD was printed in 1744 when I was turning 37. Join me in proclaiming His wonderful name without ceasing!

    For you are also God's servant.

                                                            Charles Wesley
                                                             (1707-1788)

Pentecost 6   Joachim Neander

Dear Saints in Christ,

    Many years ago I served with Pastor Theodore Under-Eyck at St. Martin's Reformed Church in Bremen, Germany. However, my time of service to him and to the Church was cut short as I passed from life to Life at an early age.

    I contracted tuberculosis by the time I was thirty years old. At only thrity, I was dying. Nevertheless, God made His strength perfect in my weakness and gave me an extra measure of faith at that time.

    If it had not been for Reverend Under-Eyck, I may well have carried on in my ungodly ways. For in my youth I led a rather "carefree" lifestyle, to say the least. I never thought about my Savior and His Church. However, with the guidance of this patient pastor, I changed my ways.

    After my behavior changed, I settled down as a tutor and teacher. During my last five years, I was an unordained assistant at St. Martin's.

    It was during this time that I also began to write hymns. I wrote approximately sixty of them. However, I do have a very favorite one, which is PRAISE TO THE LORD, THE ALMIGHTY. At the time I wrote it, I asked that it be sung with its familiar tune. As far as I know, it has never been sung to any other melody.

    I had one regret about dying at an early age. I would have liked to have written more hymns. However, my family didn't understand my journey of faith ... my hymnwriting. They only ridiculed me. In return, I prayed for them.

    Glorify God. Without Him, you have nothing. With Him, you have everything, although it may not seem to be that way when you find yourselves in pain and suffering.

> *Praise to the Lord, the Almighty, the King of creation!*
> *O my soul, praise him, for he is your health and salvation!*
> *Let all who hear*

*Now to his temple draw near,
Joining in glad adoration!*

I beg you, praise the Lord with me!

Joachim Neander
(1650-1680)

Pentecost 7   **Horatius Bonar**

Dear People of Christ,

It surely is a joy for you to come to church to worship our God. Do you by any chance ask your neighbors and friends?

"Come." That was the word I said to all I ever met, whether they belonged to my parish or whether I met them while traveling. I not only said it, I printed it, giving pamphlets out to people. I wanted everyone to know the love of Jesus.

Born into a Scottish family, my two brothers and I entered the ministry. Our family had been active in the Church of Scotland for over two centuries. During my ministry, there was a revolution within the church. As a result hundreds of the ministers left, forming the Free Church of Scotland.

Even before ordination in 1837, I was busy assisting in one of the churches at Leith. This church was in a poor neighborhood. As I helped with Sunday School, I noticed that the children did not like to sing the psalms. Consequently, I began to write my own Sunday School songs, setting them to familiar tunes of the day, much as Martin Luther did. The result was that the children now loved to sing!

I continued my ministry after ordination, taking over the parish of my father-in-law in Kelso. I had married his daughter, Jane Lundie. For forty years our marriage blossomed in joy and despite the sorrow. We lost five wee ones to death. But Jane and I still clung to our faith and to each other.

Known as the "Prince of Scottish Hymns," I wrote around 600. It's hard for me to believe that 100 are still in use today. For they had already gone around the world in my time. I drifted away from the practice of metrical psalms to *hymns* of faith and praise. Perhaps my most famous one is I HEARD THE VOICE OF JESUS SAY. Now just what does He say?

"Come."

Horatius Bonar
(1808-1889)

Pentecost 8 — Johann Franck

Dear Friends of Christ,

I lived through the Thirty Years' War in Germany like many others. But the war did not affect me nearly as much as some of my contemporaries. This did not mean, however, that my life was lived out in perfect tranquility.

When I was two, my father died. Oh! How I wished as a boy and as a man to have known Father. For who can replace a father's love? Who can replace another person? Each one of us is a unique creation made in God's image. There will never be another person like you. Or even like me.

However, my uncle did adopt me, and saw to it that I received a good education at the University of Koenigsberg. Like my father, my uncle was a lawyer. At Koenigsberg, I followed in their footsteps, taking up this profession.

My greatest accomplishment was not related to being a lawyer or even to the positions which I held. I am primarily remembered for my poetry.

Even though I wrote secular poems, it is my poetry for the Church that has endured to this very day. The 110 hymns which I penned far outrank anything else I achieved during my lifetime. JESU, MEINE FREUDE or JESUS, MY JOY* is the most well-known.

Each of us is a joy and treasure to God. But the Joy of joys is Christ. No amount of money could ever purchase the treasure of his love on Good Friday. Martin Luther summed it up this way:

> *At great cost*
> *he has saved and redeemed me*
> *A lost and condemned person.*
> *He has freed me*
> *from sin, death, and the power of the devil —*
> *not with silver or gold*
> *but with his holy and precious blood*
> *and his innocent suffering and death.***

Most people consider their joy to be the treasures of wealth and affluence. However, the *secret* of real joy is that you cannot buy it. My greatest treasure as a lawyer? Jesus, my joy.

What is your treasure?

Johann Franck
(1618-1677)

* The English version is known as JESUS, PRICELESS TREASURE.

** Reprinted from *The Small Catechism in Contemporary English* by Martin Luther. Copyright © 1960, 1968 Augsburg Publishing House. Used by permission of Augsburg Fortress.

Pentecost 9 **Carl Gustaf Boberg**

Dear Members of Christ,

It is the beautiful summertime again. What an opportunity to praise our God when we see the beauty God has bestowed upon the earth. The sunshine, the plains, the mountains, the flourishing green grass and the creation of the flowers from the bud to the flower in full bloom.

Although I lived in a scenic spot in Sweden, I took it all for granted. Many of us do that at one time or another. Seeing the charming countryside all the time, I thought nothing of its beauty. Then one summer day we had a thunderstorm. This was not unusual.

I had been out visiting. Upon returning home, the sun came out in the early evening. The birds were singing. I saw the grass in the countryside embellished with flowers sparkling in the sunlight. I smelled the freshness of the rain. I heard the bells ringing with joy from the spires of churches. It was as if I were tasting creation itself. I was absolutely awe-inspired.

Coming home, I knew I had to put on paper what was in my heart. The greatness of our God! Out of the thunderstorm, my senses came alive. The hymn, HOW GREAT THOU ART, stirred in my heart on my journey home.

God had opened another world to me in His wondrous creation. A scene of grandeur rose to meet me as I walked. Having at last reached home, I began penning the words to this hymn.

I set out in life being a sailor, but I experienced a "conversion." Out of that experience, I eventually became a lay preacher in my hometown. I also was a writer, speaker, and editor of a weekly newspaper, finally becoming a member of the Swedish parliament.

Sing with Christians around the world HOW GREAT THOU ART.

From the depths of your heart.

Carl Gustaf Boberg
(1850-1940)

Pentecost 10   **John Ernest Bode**

Dear Ones in Christ,

How good it is to keep in touch with you, the communion of saints. I always kept in touch with Christians as rector in the Anglican Church in England. Unlike my father, who was head of the foreign department of the post office, I chose to make a lifelong commitment to the Church as a clergyman.

Receiving my Master of Arts degree in 1840 from Christ College, Oxford, I was ordained the following year. I only had two parishes in my lifetime. In the first one, I served as rector at Westwell, Oxfordshire, in 1847. Thirteen years later, I moved to the parish of Castle Camps, Cambridgeshire, where I held the same position.

In addition to serving the Anglican Church as a priest, I loved to write. Three of my books were published during my life. They were *Ballads from Herodotus* (1853), *Short Occasional Poems* (1858), and *Hymns from the Gospel of the Day, for Each Sunday and the Festivals of Our Lord* (1860).

My hymn, O JESUS, I HAVE PROMISED, originally read O JESUS, WE HAVE PROMISED. I wrote in it 1866 on the occasion of the confirmation of my daughter and two sons. It is based on the text found in Saint Luke 9:57, "I will follow You wherever You go."

Do you remember the promise you made when you were confirmed to be faithful to our Lord? Perhaps time has dimmed your commitment. Perhaps time has erased the Bible passage you were given at the time of your confirmation.

Look for the passage if you can't remember what it was. But most importantly, renew in your heart the promise of faithfulness you made to Christ on the day you were confirmed. He has remembered His promises to you.

Have you remembered your promise to Him?

                                                               John Ernest Bode
                                                                  (1816-1874)

Pentecost 11 — Georg Neumark

Dear People of Christ,

    I am writing this letter to encourage you to be steadfast in your faith. At the end of my life my eyes became cloudy. I was robbed of my sight. But being robbed was nothing new to me.

    As a young man, I was riding in a coach on my way to the university in Koenigsberg. All of a sudden near Magdeburg, bandits came out from hiding and jumped our carriage. I was robbed. After the incident, I possessed only my prayer book and some money which had been sewn in my pocket.

    I was devastated. Just devastated, I tell you. All of my hopes and dreams disappeared within thirty minutes. I walked from city to city trying to find employment. But there was none. After my attempts, a pastor in Kiel found me a position as tutor to a Judge Henning's family. Yes, I was grateful, but I knew my dream of going to university was still far away.

    After two years, I was able to make the journey to the University of Koenigsberg once more. After studying poetry as well as law, I made my home in Weimar, serving one of the dukes.

    In the end, it was my poetry that led me to declare my faith in God. I wrote approximately 34 hymns, but perhaps my most famous one is IF YOU BUT TRUST IN GOD TO GUIDE YOU.

    You know, I wrote the text and the tune for this hymn when I was only in my early twenties, during the time I was tutor to the children of Judge Henning. It was such a relief to find work. I knew God was guiding me.

    Yes, I've been there too. When I was robbed as a young man. When I was robbed of my sight. But there's one thing no one ever robbed me of ...

    My eyes of steadfast faith.

Georg Neumark
(1621-1681)

Pentecost 12   **Bates Burt**

Dear Youth in Christ,

    The purpose of this letter is to encourage you in many things. In the gift of your faith and the talents which God has given you. I am also challenging you to use both in the opportunities which lie before you as your journey continues.

    I used my faith and the gifts which God bestowed upon me. This led me to wonderful opportunities. The results stretched out far beyond my lifetime and in places which I never dreamed.

    I received a good education. By 1902, I was a deacon in the Episcopal church. The following year, I became a priest. For most of my life, I served two parishes in Michigan. One was in Marquette and the other in Pontiac.

    In addition, I composed both words and music for hymns and Christmas carols. O GOD OF YOUTH was used for several high school baccalaureate services. Later, I wrote a new tune for this text. I named the new tune *Lynne* for my first grandchild. The text with its new tune was included in the 1940 *Episcopal Hymnal.* This was followed by its acceptance in other hymnbooks just for you, our young people.

    You see, I had a wonderful family. God blessed us with three children. Our youngest son, Alfred, was a born musician. I encouraged him in his natural talent. Our family sent out original musical Christmas cards. At first I wrote the music and words. In 1942, I handed the composition of these carols over to Al.

    I would have never dreamed that the "Alfred Burt Christmas Carols" would be sung and played around the world every year. Even by the Boston Pops Orchestra! They shine with words of faith, hope, and love. The lyrics were written by myself and later by our former organist, Wihla Hutson. Teamed up with the beauty found in Al's compositions, these carols have a unique place in the music of Christmas.

The Christ Child was a youth. He has been where you are now. Where I once was. He will give you that encouragement to let your faith and talent shine.

More than you can ever know.

Bates Burt
(1878-1948)

Pentecost 13　　　　　　　　　　Karolina Wilhelmina Berg

Dear Children in Christ,

Do you realize that you are always a child of our Heavenly Father? All through my life, I felt the presence of that Father.

My life was woven with many different threads ... illness, a miracle, grief, creativity, a husband. But through it all, God, my Heavenly Father, was always with there for me.

When I was a child, I was diagnosed with crippling paralysis — supposedly incurable. One Sunday my earthly father, Pastor Jonas Sandell, held worship at his Lutheran church as usual. Mother naturally went also. Only twelve, I spent that morning in prayer. By the time they came home, a miracle had occurred. I was dressed and walking about. They were absolutely amazed. What a happy scene!

I wrote already as a youngster. I felt a loving warmth from my parents as well as the radiant loving presence of God when I was paralyzed. This love remained with me as I journeyed through life. I penned CHILDREN OF THE HEAVENLY FATHER.

I saw my father drown right in front of my eyes when I was 26. My heart — oh, you will never know — how my heart drowned in grief at the very same moment. By the fall of that same year, my mother also died. Now I had only my Heavenly Father.

But He supplied my daily wants and needs. I kept in constant touch with Him as His child. By doing so, He directed my path. In 1867, I married a Stockholm merchant and helped him with his literary work.

During the last half of the nineteenth century I became Sweden's greatest hymnwriter, or so it has been said. My whole collection of poems was published between 1882-1892. There were 650.

Even though I grew older, I always felt in my heart that I was a child of the Heavenly Father.

Like Jesus.

　　　　　　　　　　　　　　　　　　Karolina Wilhelmina Berg
　　　　　　　　　　　　　　　　　　　　　(1832-1903)

Pentecost 14　　　　　　　　　　　　　　**Horatio G. Spafford**

Beloved Ones in Christ,

I am writing you this letter to tell you about the tragedy that led to my trip from Chicago to Wales in the last weeks of 1873. I wanted to rejoin my dear wife there. Here's what happened.

On the advice of our physician, I sent my wife to Europe for her health. Our four daughters also went with her on the ship, the *S.S. Ville du Havre*. I was to have gone along with them, taking a break from my law practice. However, at the last minute, I had to remain behind in Chicago.

During their voyage, the *S.S. du Ville Havre* was struck by another ship on November 22. Within twelve minutes, the *S.S. du Ville Havre* carrying my wife and daughters sank. In just twelve short minutes, we lost our four darling girls.

Thank God, my wife survived. It was during the voyage to meet her in Wales when I wrote WHEN PEACE, LIKE A RIVER. I cannot tell you how my heart ached for my girls. I cannot begin to share the grief I experienced.

"Why my daughters?" I asked. I could only find peace in my merciful Savior. No one else could comfort my "why." Perhaps you, too, are struggling with a "why" in your life.

Generation upon generation have asked "why." The only answer, the only peace, can be found in the Prince of Peace, Christ Himself.

I know.

When peace, like a river, attendeth my way;
When sorrows, like sea billows, roll;
Whatever my lot, Thou hast taught me to say,
It is well, it is well with my soul.

　　　　　　　　　　　　　　　　Horatio G. Spafford
　　　　　　　　　　　　　　　　(1828-1888)

Pentecost 15   **John Douglas Sutherland Campbell**

My dear Friends in Christ,

I lived in eastern Canada, where I served as Governor General. As I saw more and more of the countryside, I never ceased to marvel at what a beautiful country God has given you. Furthermore, I understand that splendor beyond description is found in the West.

I came from England in 1878 with my dear wife, Princess Louise Alberta. Actually, the Province of Alberta and its famous Lake Louise were named after my wife. In Canada, I represented my mother-in-law, our gracious Queen Victoria.

When I was in Canada, UNTO THE HILLS took on a far greater meaning to me. As I surveyed the landscape around me, I surely saw God's "grand design."

And certainly, you people in the West with the mountains must be moved every day when you cast your glance up to the heavens. UNTO THE HILLS is based on Psalm 121, which you may want to read and to pray whether there are mountains surrounding you or not.

Take heart in whatever troubles you see yourself. Keep looking up to our Lord just as you people in the West look up to those peaks. For you will find His strong arms encircling you.

With His mighty shoulders for you to rest upon.

> *Unto the hills around do I lift up*
> *My longing eyes;*
> *Oh, whence for me shall my salvation come,*
> *From whence arise?*
> *From God the Lord doth come my certain aid,*
> *From God the Lord, who heav'n and earth hath made.*

                                             John Douglas Sutherland Campbell
                                                            (1845-1914)

Pentecost 16 — Benjamin Schmolck

Dear People in Christ Jesus,

I always loved the Church, the communion of saints, as well as the spires that dotted my country of Germany. Curious, I opened many church doors.

Here I found beauty in the colors of the stained glass windows, in the furnishings, in the ornate silver chalice, and in the mighty sound of the pipes of the organ. But more importantly, I found God in His earthly house.

I knew in my formative years that I wanted to hold the same position as my father. I wanted to be a Lutheran pastor and nothing else! When I was only sixteen, I preached my first sermon.

I thoroughly enjoyed the experience. And Father's church members seemed to like my preaching. So much so in fact that one member gave me a study allowance for three years to pursue theology. You might say I was a born preacher. This was a gift to me from the Lord.

However, by my final year in university, the study allowance had been used up. The question of how I would pay for this year loomed like a large dark cloud. Then I had an idea. I could support myself by writing. I wrote much of my poetry for the Church. During my lifetime, I penned approximately 1,000 hymns! At 25 years of age, I was crowned *poet laureate*.

Soon after, I was ordained as Father's assistant. However, my biggest challenge came later when two other pastors and I ministered to 36 villages having only one church! I was always busy. Always preaching.

At times I was just exhausted. It was at such moments that I glanced over the text of my hymn, OPEN NOW THY GATES OF BEAUTY. Having gone to the heavenly Kingdom, I can tell you that the radiant beauty is beyond words.

Someday you *will* see as you pass the gates.

Benjamin Schmolck
(1672-1737)

Pentecost 17   **William Williams**

My dear Ones in Christ,

I cannot even begin to tell you how much I loved to write hymns. Some 900 flowed from my pen. The majority, 800, were written in Welsh, while the others were written in English.

Starting out in life, I wanted to study medicine. However, when I heard the preaching of Howell Harris (an associate of George Whitefield) I was inspired by his message. So inspired that I, too, wanted to become a leader in the Church. I was ordained as a deacon in the Church of England.

However, it wasn't long after this that I became involved with the evangelistic movement under the influence of the Methodists. I felt it was my "calling" to be just that. An evangelist.

For the next 45 years, Wales became my parish as I traveled 3,000 miles every year to share the Gospel. My dear wife was a singer. She accompanied me on numerous trips as I crisscrossed the landscape of Wales.

Winning a hymnwriting contest, I was soon recognized for this talent with which God blessed me. In Wales, I am known as the Isaac Watts of England or the Paul Gerhardt of Germany. GUIDE ME EVER, GREAT REDEEMER was written for the people of Wales in their native language. It appeared in my *Alleluia,* printed in 1745 when I was in my late twenties.

John Hughes wrote its current melody in the early part of the twentieth century for a Welsh singing festival. *Cwm Rhondda* translates as the "valley of the Rhondda," as the river *Rhondda* is found there. Both are located in the heart of the coal mining industry in Wales.

GUIDE ME EVER, GREAT REDEEMER, now in 75 languages, is still spreading God's marvelous message just as I did once so many years ago.

Wouldn't you agree?

                                                      William Williams
                                                         (1717-1791)

Pentecost 18 — George Croly

Dear Friends in the Spirit of Christ,

It is good to join you in the Spirit of God today. I always asked for God's counsel during my life. It is the best wisdom to be found anywhere. The Holy Spirit, the best teacher.

I was born and educated in Dublin, Ireland. Ordained into the Church of Ireland (Anglican), I went to London in 1810. There I pursued literary activities. I wrote in many forms ... drama, poetry, novels, as well as satire.

I also ministered to two churches in the city, St. Benet in Sherehob and St. Stephen's in Walbrook. St. Stephen's was located in one of London's worst slums. All the way from the culture of London, which I encountered while writing, to the wretched living conditions found at Walbrook.

While I was at St. Stephen's, I saw to it that the pulpit was rebuilt. There had been no preaching of God's Holy Word from one for over a century! With the pulpit in place and the Lord's gracious help, I enthusiastically preached sermons which attracted many people to St. Stephen's.

While in my seventies, there was a need for a new hymnal. Accepting a challenge, I prepared one myself. SPIRIT OF GOD, DESCEND UPON MY HEART was listed beneath the heading "Holiness Desired" in my *Psalms and Hymns for Public Worship*. Other hymns of mine were included in this songbook as well. Thirteen years later, SPIRIT OF GOD, DESCEND UPON MY HEART appeared in a hymnal prepared by Charles Rogers. The hymn was on the move, "descending" into the community of faith.

No matter where I was or what my age, I felt that the Holy Spirit was always counseling me and teaching me. Teaching me to feel that God was always near, to bear the struggles of my faith, to be patient in prayer, to love Him as I ought.

To give my heart as an altar to Him.

George Croly
(1780-1860)

Pentecost 19   **William Walsham How**

Dear People in Christ,

In later years, I held the office of Bishop. At times I was known as "the children's bishop" because I loved them dearly. Queen Victoria appointed me Bishop of Bedford. The territory I served included the slums of East London. I ministered to the very poor. There I was known as "the poor man's bishop." Identifying with my people as much as I could, I took the bus rather than riding in carriages like other bishops. Because of this I was also known as "the omnibus bishop." Finally, as Bishop of Wakefield, I became involved with England's laborers, the factory workers.

As Bishop, I carried a shepherd's staff. On it I engraved the words, *Pasce verbo, pasce vita,* or "Feed with the Word, feed with Life." Just one of the many sayings handed down to the Church by Saint Bernard of Clairvaux.

We all need God's Word on our path in life. But especially as Bishop, I needed God's Word to feed me. For I was shepherding very large flocks at times.

But all along in my ministry, even as that curate in a farming village, I knew I needed God's Word to sustain me on my journey through life. I hungered for Christ, the Bread of Life. Having received my spiritual nourishment, I was satisfied. O WORD OF GOD INCARNATE is a prayer that all may know Jesus, our Savior, by grazing on God's Word.

The food found in the Bible is like no other. Would you like this food on your journey through life? All you have to do is open the holy book. Here you will find Christ Himself who became incarnate, who lived on earth.

That we might dwell with Him in heaven.

                                         William Walsham How
                                                 (1823-1897)

Pentecost 20   **Martin Rinckart**

My dear Friends in Christ, our Lord,

I remember when the raging Thirty Years' War ended. I never ceased to give thanks for blessed peace! While the war waged on, people fled to our city, Eilenberg, for protection. You see, it was surrounded by a large wall.

Times grew tough. Although the war was far from over, I had, by that time, already seen enough. The war was ugly. Horrible. All I could do was pray. As I look back, things only grew worse.

My wife and I took in many refugee families who came here. I tell you, sometimes I did not know where I was going to put them or what I was going to feed them. But somehow, God gave me His eyes. I just could not turn these families away.

It was during this same time, in 1636, that the table prayer which I wrote for my children came into print. NOW THANK WE ALL OUR GOD was a prayer for my children to pray before the noonday meal.

You may not think there was anything for which to give thanks, but we did have food and shelter, although meager. But most importantly, we had Christ who had gone all the way to the Cross for all victims of this horrid war.

As the years passed, Eilenberg became dirty and overcrowded. The pestilence was also raging. During 1637, two Lutheran pastors died. That same year, the senior church official decided to move out of the utter devastation. This left me to minister to the city by myself.

My wife died. At times, I buried up to seventy people in one day. I would have never survived the wretchedness going on around me if it had not been for my Savior.

If you are facing tough times, turn to Christ. For He will never let you down. Thank God, He is there for you. Just as He was for me. Always.

                                                   Martin Rinckart
                                                     (1586-1649)

Pentecost 21   **Matthias Claudius**

Dear People in Christ,

I was brought up in a Lutheran parsonage in Germany. Going off to university, I held to the faith of my youth. However, it was when I came into contact with Rationalistic thinkers of the time that my views began to change. I drifted away from Christ. Rationalism was appealing. It was the latest craze.

Self-improvement was all the rage. Keeping the body in shape was "in" as well as caring for the environment. These ideas are not bad in and of themselves. But they became "gods." Meanwhile, virtue was translated for the word that we call piety. The phrase "a better life" replaced the word "heaven." God was fate.

And if this was not enough, editors began deleting hymns referring to Christ, and hymnwriters themselves left His Name out of hymns. Congregations sang rhymed hymns on immortality. Thinking nothing of this change, I "bought" into this mode of thought. It was *very* easy to get caught up in this ... just about everyone was into this "new age."

Later in life, severe illness struck me. After the worst was over, I began to reflect. In doing so, *I returned to the faith of my youth.* While the qualities of Rationalism sounded good, they are of no comfort when you are ill. Even possibly dying. Christ had sought me out, for I was that one lost sheep.

I was a journalist during my lifetime. A hymn eventually came out of a poem I wrote titled "Paul Erdmann's Feast." WE PLOW THE FIELDS AND SCATTER is the song of the peasants in the poem. In their singing, they are praising God for ultimately being the source of the feast.

Help scatter the Word, won't you? An "age" like Rationalism comes and goes, but Christ and His Church are here to stay. Take some advice from me, don't get caught up in an "age."

I know. I've been there.

                                                            Matthias Claudius
                                                               (1740-1815)

**Reformation Sunday
(Pentecost 22)**

Nikolai Grundtvig

Dear People of Christ,

Some have referred to me as the greatest Danish hymnwriter of the nineteenth century. I am very humbled. However, without the Lord's help, my life would not have been woven with the beautiful threads of His protecting love.

As the son of a Lutheran pastor, I attended university where I encountered the Rationalists. Although I fell under their influence for a time, it wasn't long until I found myself in opposition to them.

Several years after graduating, I received a message from my father. He was ill and was in need of an assistant. I went back to Udby in 1810 and preached my trial sermon for ordination. I did not preach what was "politically correct" at the time, for I confronted the Rationalists right in this sermon.

I paid dearly for my words. Because I was true to the Gospel, my ordination was delayed for a whole year! During the next ten years I wasn't given a parish. In fact, I wasn't even allowed to confirm my own children!

However, as time went on, my preaching was blessed, as was the poetry that flowed from my pen such as BUILT ON A ROCK. By 1839, I was fully reinstated as a clergyman.

God blessed me abundantly for the rest of my life, and in the end the King of Denmark appointed me a bishop. I was faithful to my Savior just as He was faithful to me. I preached my last sermon *the day* before I died, just days before my eighty-ninth birthday.

Our God *is* faithful.

Nikolai Grundtvig
(1783-1872)

**All Saints' Sunday
(Pentecost 23)**

John Athelstan Laurie Riley

Dear Saints in Christ,

As one of the editors of the *English Hymnal* of 1906, I wrote these words for the tune *Lasst uns erfreuen*. I thought this tune should have a "heavenly" text. By the time I had finished YE WATCHERS AND YE HOLY ONES, I felt these words were right for the melody.

Interested in translating Latin and Greek, I received two degrees from Pembroke College at Oxford. Later in my travels, I visited the Eastern world. I went off to faraway lands such as Persia, Turkey, and Kurdistan.

Out of my experiences there, I published brochures as well as articles on the Christian Church in the East. And because of these same experiences, I wrote YE WATCHERS AND YE HOLY ONES as eastern Christians worship.

You see, there is a difference between worshiping God in the West and in the East. In the West, God comes down to us on our level, just as He came down to earth at Christmas.

On the other hand, the eastern Christians ascend to the very heights of heaven, joining the angels in their worship. Eastern Christians are "watching," so to speak, just as the disciples long ago watched. With eyes uplifted they saw Jesus, the King of Kings, as He ascended into heaven.

Look for this type of eastern "imagery" in what many consider to be a "holy hymn" in quest of the eternal. Christ, the Lamb of God in the eternal kingdom ... My quest has been fulfilled, for now I worship and adore Jesus with the angels without end.

Have you given this scene much thought lately?

John Athelstan Laurie Riley
(1858-1945)

Pentecost 24 **Johann Michael Altenberg**

Dear People of Christ,

I was born on Trinity Sunday close to Erfurt in Germany. How well I knew the city. However, Erfurt changed in the 54 years before I returned as pastor of St. Andrew's Lutheran Church.

During the time in between, so many people including myself lived through the horrid Thirty Years' War. Really, you cannot imagine what war is like unless you have lived through one. Praise God if you have never had the experience.

Innocent, loving people that were alive before the war began were dead after the war was over. Victims. I prayed for them as well as for myself.

However, I also prayed for all of us not to be afraid when warring troops surrounded us. What good would it do? Although there was much to fear, we knew God was our Shepherd in all of this misery.

In 1631 I heard of the victory of the Protestant forces in Leipzig. I wrote DO NOT DESPAIR LITTLE FLOCK as a prayer of reassurance.

I could not let fear grip me. What good would that do? Would fear give me a longer life? Would fear be of any help to me? Obviously not. I wanted people to know this.

The next year, my hymn became the "swan song" for the Swedish King, Gustavus Adolphus. You see, during the course of the war, Sweden had been asked to join our forces to let Lutherans and Protestants flourish in Germany.

Before the battle at Luetzen in November 1632, the "Snow King" commanded that his army sing DO NOT DESPAIR LITTLE FLOCK. Then, Gustavus Adolphus knelt in prayer. As the battle began, the King was mortally wounded. But he was not afraid. This was the turning point. The evangelical cause was assured of staying.

Thank God wars are not fought anymore over the Christian faith. While there is no perfect unity, *all* Christians belong to the Good Shepherd. We are *one* in His kingdom.

Now that's "Good News!"

Johann Michael Altenberg
(1584-1640)